Temple Garden

"With Jock Stein, we are on pilgrimage through the world and our own hearts. In one moment, we 'gaze aghast at Abraham's warring children,' the next, we are in our backyards to 'wake, remember who I am.' . . . Soaring heights and local depths are captured in 'Incarnation,' which is a meditation on the God who bridges these extremes, as do Stein's poems for us in this short and absolutely lovely book where God tells us to 'read my lips.'"

—**Julie Canlis**, Liturgical Director, Trinity Church, Washington State

"Jock Stein applies his keen poetic ear, and knowledge of poetic form, to his understanding of Scripture and theology to create poems of depth and integrity. The book's subtitle, *Poems of Faith and Curiosity*, is particularly apt as it contains many poems in which Stein wrestles honestly and unflinchingly with the big questions. But there is also humor and hope and a warm appreciation of relationships, of nature, and human creativity."

—**Christine De Luca**, poet and former Edinburgh Makar

"There's much beauty being fought for in these poems. . . . The wrestling is not only done with ideas and what we face today in terms of environmental chaos and our loss of God; it's also with history, with what Scotland was and where she stands today. What I will carry with me is the raw honesty of these journeys of thought, these finely-honed meditations where every word has been weighed."

—**Kenneth Steven**, poet

"*Temple Garden* is full of sights and sounds, . . . a landscape where divine love is at the center and the circumference, a world where revelation, history, politics and plants coexist through beautiful words and imagery. . . . It is an inspiring anthology, a haven for questioning minds, wounded souls, and lovers of beauty."

—**Murray Watts**, author and director of *The Wayfarer Trust*

"This poetic coat of many colors shows us that faith and curiosity are cut from the same cloth—wondering at God's creation, wrestling with its despoiling, witnessing to its glory. These are classic Jock Stein poems to make us think, taking ourselves less seriously, but taking us to the heart of the matter. We are alive in God's garden of delight but always weeding the hard questions. Put on this shimmering coat when you do."

—**William Storrar**, Director, Princeton Center for Theological Inquiry

"*Temple Garden* gathers singular works [of poetry], each one both a praise-song and an argument, a hymn to creation's magnitude and a prayer for her vulnerability. . . . Stein's faith is Christian, but his range of sympathetic reference is much broader than any single church, and if his poetry might challenge the pieties of reverence, it never for a moment loses its sense of respect for humankind's capacity to love and be renewed."

—**Alan Riach**, Professor of Scottish Literature, University of Glasgow

Temple Garden

Poems of Faith and Curiosity

Jock Stein

RESOURCE *Publications* · Eugene, Oregon

TEMPLE GARDEN
Poems of Faith and Curiosity

Copyright © 2025 Jock Stein. All rights reserved. Except for brief quotations in critical publications or reviews, no part of this book may be reproduced in any manner without prior written permission from the publisher. Write: Permissions, Wipf and Stock Publishers, 199 W. 8th Ave., Suite 3, Eugene, OR 97401.

Resource Publications
An Imprint of Wipf and Stock Publishers
199 W. 8th Ave., Suite 3
Eugene, OR 97401

www.wipfandstock.com

PAPERBACK ISBN: 979-8-3852-4662-5
HARDCOVER ISBN: 979-8-3852-4663-2
EBOOK ISBN: 979-8-3852-4664-9
VERSION NUMBER 08/26/25

Contents

Introduction *by Harry Smart*

Temple Garden (Psalm 1) | 1

Nature
Night | 3
Swift (Matthew 10 v.29) | 4
Woodland Philosophy | 5
Beech in Sunshine | 6
Blue in Flodigarry | 7
Director's Cut | 8
The Dyfi Estuary | 9
Breath of Hope | 10
Who's Listening? | 11
Monument | 12

Scotland
Miracles | 13
St Mary's Haddington at Night | 14
Saltire | 15
Luik til the Burds o the Lift (Matthew 6 v.26) | 16
How Things Are | 17
Tones of Destiny | 18
Inchcolm | 20

In Response to Bible Texts
Incarnation (Psalm 138 v.6) | 21
Beating on the Door (Psalm 13 v.1) | 22
Shepherd Sonnet (Psalm 23) | 23
Enemies (Psalm 35 v.1) | 24
The Cosmic Synagogue (Psalm 41 vv.8–9) | 25

v

Longing (Psalm 84) | 27
Fair and Square (Psalm 119) | 28
A Proverb Reconsidered (Proverbs 6 v.6) | 29
The Golden Rule (Matthew 7 v.12) | 30
The Father's Hands (Luke 15 vv.11–32) | 31
The Lord's Breakfast (John 21 vv.1–13) | 32
Swimming Lessons from Gaza (Romans 4 v.20) | 33
The Hourglass (1 Corinthians 10 v.4) | 34
Change (Revelation 21) | 35
Scent from Patmos (Revelation 1 vv.9–20) | 37

Questions
Consequences | 39
Bible Shopping | 40
Celebrating Life | 41
Discovery | 42
Do Not Put 'Gentle' onto God | 43
Reaching for It | 44
God Chatter | 46
Mind Maps | 48

Poems of Time And Season
Nothing Much | 49
Coincidence | 50
Advent | 51
Advent Thoughts | 52
Epiphany | 53
Holy Saturday | 54
The End of It | 55
Old | 56
Fresh | 57
Heaven to Go | 58
Sky Talk | 60
Occupation | 61

Notes | 62
Acknowledgments | 64

Introduction
by Harry Smart

The title poem of Jock Stein's collection is a natural doorway into the whole. 'Temple Garden' points to faith, but not a single faith. We find ourselves in synagogue, mosque and Christian church in these poems.

Many respond to specific biblical texts—some of these reflect Stein's doctoral work on the psalms which considers their appropriation by believer and unbeliever alike, and in which Stein wrote poems in response to all 150 psalms. The texts in this collection range across both the Jewish Bible and the Christian New Testament. Aside from the biblical text there are poems in which faith confronts the modern world, the natural world, the world of science, and conflict.

For Christians 'garden' evokes the early chapters of Genesis. In Stein's work we are "outside Eden, sour-soiled farms make cultivation toil and pain". Two more archetypal gardens are evoked, Gethsemane and the city of the book of Revelation, which is itself a garden.

A garden is more. It's a pleasance, a place of quiet, of light on the leaves of trees and of birdsong; a safe place to relax. A garden is a place of work; Stein finds "God in shirtsleeves" there. Then there is the garden which is the natural world, with its vast networked ecosystems. A garden where soils are soured, where cities encroach on green spaces, where climate change brings drought.

Temples and gardens are *made* spaces, constructions that can be destroyed and then remade. Stein speaks of creation as God's "risky story". God's children can choose, and even a beech tree has agency. One way to think of Stein's poetry is as the mapping of the world and the damage to it that must precede repair. History, in Stein's poetry, has both genesis and telos. We stand in a ruined city but look forward to a new. This sets Stein in the Augustinian tradition: *City of God* opens with Rome fallen, its survivors broken; there is no way back, only the imperative of making new. Stein maps the world as battlefield, as woodland, as genome and as promise.

There are poisons in gardens, and venom. In *Swimming Lessons from Gaza* Stein confronts the violent legacy of faith, of "Abraham's warring children claiming that the pool they fill with blood is theirs alone."

The title poem has a clear counterpart in *The Cosmic Synagogue*. The poem is a response to Psalm 41: "A deadly thing has fastened on me . . . even my bosom friend has lifted the heel against me." Jock Stein is a formalist and *The Cosmic Synagogue* is a sestina; in each stanza a line ends with 'snake'. This synagogue has "human snakes"; people of faith "play racist cards with snakes"; 'Amen' can be hissed as easily as spoken reverently.

This is poetry in the great Scots tradition. Stein is a makar: it's the Scots word we use for poets in the workmanlike tradition of *making*, as the word 'poetry' itself once was, derived from *poiesis*, Greek for making.

There is a tradition in Scots poetry of flyting. Two poets challenge one another in a contest of wit and invention; it can be a bitter exchange; insults can be personal and sharp, but nobody flytes with a lesser talent; flyting is a mark of respect. Stein's poetry flytes with God. Hard challenges, though never insulting. Alongside flyting there's something Sufism calls *sohbet*: it can simply mean conversation, but in conversation with God it can be a quarrel.

We cannot censor these conversations. We must confront frankly the violence of the world, the violent legacy of faith, and the apparent absence of God. Nor can we ignore the world's beauty, and Stein is aware of it, and of its sensuality. In *The Cosmic Synagogue* he admits that "to hold together different worlds is hard, to keep believing humming birds and snakes both share a cosmic plan."

Theodicy is central to this poetry collection, but not as an abstract philosophical consideration; it is physical, as in *Beating on the Door*. It's a response to Psalm 13, "How long, O Lord? Will you forget me forever?" Theodicy is passionate, physical, even life-threatening: "I will ooze death from every pore while casually the Devil rips my fading faith to shreds." In the poem Stein derides 'glib' faith, charismatic 'cantrips'—a Scots word for magical spells that becomes a word for trickery, for clever half-truths or *letheia*—the deliberate forgetting against which John, in the opening of his gospel, declares Christ to stand in contrast.

Stein tackles glib faith head on in *The Golden Rule*. He scorns "those who polish up the golden rule until they see their own reflection shining at them". That cheapened faith doesn't listen, doesn't feel another's pain, has no time for questions or radical enquiry. It's a faith that, in *Bible Shopping*, "wants a simple God of love"; it wants nothing of "awful" books like Exodus, where God kills babies and imperial troops alike. As with the cosmic synagogue, so with its sacred books, it's hard to hold the bloody and the beautiful together.

The Scottish poems do that holding work particularly successfully. In *Inchcolm* we travel with day trippers to the island of that name in the Firth of Forth which was once used as a prisoner of war camp. Now it's a place of ruins, a home for seagulls. But this "iron ship" has a chapter house, and when the tourists are gone, there is a "testament of earth and angels, everywhere a memory of holiness".

The Scottish flag, the Saltire, in the poem of that title, is made in the blue sky by two planes crossing, perhaps F-35s, their crews training for war. Scotland's history has often been violent; when it has enjoyed independence, it's had to fight for it. Stein recalls Henry de Bohun, whose head was shattered by Robert Bruce's axe at the Battle of Bannockburn.

There is only one poem wholly in Scots in the book, *Luik til the Burds o the Lift*, a title riffing on Jesus' words that we consider the sparrows and God's care for them. As Stein notes, 'lift' is Scots for air or sky, although it can be a word for heaven too. Besides that one Scots poem, Scotland's words season the book, as 'cantrips' above. There is a nod to Gaelic, one of the languages of what has been called a 'three-tongued nation'. Many of these Scots words are proper nouns. The names range across centuries of Scottish literature, from David Lindsay's sixteenth century *Ane Pleasant Satyre of the Thrie Estaitis* to the contemporary crime fiction of Ian Rankin. There are giants of science like James Clerk Maxwell, and of comedy, like Billy Connolly whose nickname, 'The Big Yin' is also a Scots expression for God. Music ranges from classical violinist Nicola Benedetti to the band Deacon Blue (Stein's connection to the band is hidden by a sleight of hand). There is Jimmy Reid who led the Clyde shipyard strikes in the 1970s, and there are names of faith like Mary Slessor who championed women's rights in Nigeria and Jane Haining who, rather than returning to safety in Scotland, stayed with the children in her Hungarian mission school, dying with them in Auschwitz.

One poem holds these themes together with especial beauty—*St Mary's Haddington at Night*. St Mary's is a pre-Reformation church. Haddington is east of Edinburgh, in the centuries-deep conflict zone between England and Scotland. It was ruined during Henry the Eighth's assault on Scotland in the sixteenth century Rough Wooing, an eight-years' war between newly-Protestant England and a Scotland with close ties to Catholic France (one of those ties being Mary Queen of Scots, later beheaded on order of Elizabeth the First). The church was only fully restored in the 1970s.

The poem is set at Candlemas. "We listen silent, scattered round the church. Candles flicker." Stein's silences are audible. The bells hang "like metal sloths, asleep". It is "a house of grace for wounded souls and worried hearts".

Stein's theodicy is worked out in a cosmic synagogue which is also a local church. It is worked out in Scotland's history, and amid the country's hope of independence. But the Scotland Stein wants is "a modest nation, wise and free". Scotland is a small nation with no ambition to dominate the world.

To return to the title poem: every garden has a gate and every temple a door. The Saltire, a St Andrew's cross in white on a blue ground, is open at all corners.

Stein's poetry has this quality of openness, of welcome, and of listening. Words for quietness are one of the collection's most recurring motifs. There is passion, even anger, but also the Christian hope of healing for the nations. *Change* responds to Revelation 21, where the New Jerusalem descends from heaven: "Adam, Eve themselves again, the poor as rich, the rich as poor, they'll cry with joy instead of pain."

We are not there yet, but it is our destination collectively and individually. So to another of the themes running through Jock Stein's collection. These are not the poems of a young man. Ahead of him is "the silent final bus" which, as he says "all poets face differently". Here's Derek Walcott in *The Prodigal*: "Do you think Time makes exceptions, do you think Death mutters, 'Maybe I'll skip this one'?" *Prodigal* is a collection from late in Walcott's life, and he knows no promise of a world to come; the women he looks at longingly are generations younger and he is alone. In *The Father's Hands* Stein also reflects on the prodigal, seeing Jesus' story from Luke's gospel mediated by Rembrandt's painting 'The Return of the Prodigal'.

Looking at the Father's two different hands resting on the Prodigal's shoulders, Stein sees "Father and mother love, combined in one whose welcome tells us all we need to know of God."

Stein is beating on a door that he is confident will open. It is, perhaps, the door that led out of Eden, guarded against Adam and Eve's return by a whirling sword. One day that sword will be sheathed, and if it isn't, these are poems that would run at the door, daring God to open it. But the way is not back, it's forward into a garden-city where God finally will dwell at peace with humankind.

Temple Garden   Psalm 1

Illuminated manuscript,
unnumbered, naming no and yes,
by some anonymous lyricist
who introduces all the rest
with contrast and with chiasm,
two parallel lines that never kiss
but cross and complicate the rhythm
of a temple garden house.

The righteous prosper, trim and trig,
manicured by God's own hand,
nourished, watered, planted snug
and safe, quite sure they know the plan.
Outside Eden, sour soiled farms
make cultivation toil and pain,
yet still enlightened by the psalms
that penetrate our dusty skin.

How simple, God's garden themes
for daily work and sabbath rest;
but underground, deep hidden genes,
our subway roots, in battle dress
keep us alive, write up our files,
assess the truth of war and peace,
press our buttons, tell us tales,
feed our choice of ant or louse.

Nature

Night

Birds sing at night for mates and heaven,
mark their pitch and search the dark
for God, to throw him *billets-doux*.
Last night I woke, took faith outside
to the dunnock fluting—or was it robin?—
world all new to me as much as Cortez,
Dvořák, any pioneer
whose door is open in the night.

Swift MATTHEW 10 V.29

They're gone from sight before my eyes can track
the sharp black flash, the headlong dash
through peaceful skies, the insect-gobbling streak
of single purpose, playful, doubling back
across my gaze. Warm summer days splash
their stuff on all my senses, every week
a new kaleidoscope of light, a loop
of string that ties a bow on everything

except the birds that never, never stop.
These artful dodgers jink and bank and swoop,
will fly a thousand miles, or dip a wing
to skiff the water, scoop a silver drop.

Now when swifts fly, the universe is cleft,
and when they fall, God counts the number left.

Woodland Philosophy

It took her fifty years to learn that pose,
to grow up wanton, give a hint
of naked provocation with that sideways
swelling of a hip—no summer clothes
to slip on hurriedly before the glint
of dawn, no shrinking from the love-struck gaze
that gardeners give: no shame, no stage fright.

Her upper arm is curved, continuing
that gorgeous trunk line, poised to flaunt
a skirt of branch lines reaching up for sky light,
running eyesight wrapt and ragged, with
a tease: "Now you see me, now you don't."

Did I place such charm within arms' reach,
or does that beauty live inside the beech?

Beech in Sunshine

Arms accelerate akimbo,
beech bare on blue,
frozen fountain of resource
and praise, today on cue
to give the world a show:
that twisted tangled limbs
may share a single source
that grows these uncut hymns
to God and nature, with no
shame in naming them
together, root and rhizome
deep in soil and say-so
to the shape of trunk and stem
and leaf and bark and poem.

Blue in Flodigarry

In Gaelic *An Taobh Sear*, The East Side
where the long sea takes the eye
at light speed over the waves, high
into the blue of the Torridon hills,

and back to Fladda—the flat island—
nose sniffing weather and water,
as curious as if we thought her
kin to fishermen and artists.

She framed her picture with two trees,
a sycamore in green regalia,
cherry pink above the azalea
—scarlet bells, a peal for praise.

A wren hopped round among the stones,
silent friend; yes, once he knew
who lived in every croft; now few
can hear the songs, and hold the tales.

Two rabbits chewed beyond the bluebells:
blue her favourite colour, like her eyes
which scanned the sea to realise
the tone of loss, an ache for heaven.

Director's Cut

She knew its hidden presence,
reached for it in her mind,
put her hands and heart there,
got down to it, to find
our image, as yet uncut
from that great lump of stone.

How could she learn to hammer
with a home grown skill
and, come to that, a chisel?

It came to this: the artist
had to occupy that rocky
place herself, and learn to dress
the stone as she herself
now dressed—in mineral wear,
plain as only God could be,
love in hardened clay laid bare.

The Dyfi Estuary

The waters wander here and there, the current
hesitates, the river takes a breath,
its energy passed out to sea,
Welsh dragon fire extinguished at low tide.
Here sandbanks rise, unfurl their necks
with golden curls, to make an ampersand
that calls each river bank to raise
a hand and greet the other. Sand formations
mirror clouds which lift and drift, bind
earth and sky, remind us that a high tide
cannot shift the low behind,
each ampersand a stealthy strand of DNA.

What is submerged when life is in full flow
will rise when dry times come, and ask, "And so?"

Breath of Hope

*"... that beautiful, beautiful, beautiful God
was breathing his love in a cut-away bog."*
(FROM 'THE ONE' BY PATRICK KAVANAGH)

Love salted with God's tears, as peat is milled
and plugs are pulled on carbon sinks,
while bogs are ruled by beautiful theology
which poets cull from colour, call from suck
and squelch of muddy boots.

Love halted in arrears, as bogs are filled
with good intentions, stable doors are shut
and firms decide to plant a hundred trees
to grow their corporate bark a ring or two,
and fake their carbon roots.

Love vaulted over years, as we rebuild
the power of breath, if we respect the bogs
and lay that three times beautiful upon our land,
while One who triples into earth and wet
keeps time, and grows new shoots.

Who's Listening?

The blue tit balances upon the fuchsia bush,
where flower pendants hang like purple ear rings.
Birds have ears, of course, and practised flight
if unexpected sound or movement springs
them into quick escape.
    But here's a secret, known
to scientists, to kings and commoners
who look for links in unexpected places:
plants can hear—sage, marigolds and firs
grow stunted close to motorways; they stress
at noise and fuss, but cherish Buddhist chant.
How blunt the modern age, to punt how clever
humans are, when all the time we can't
control our climate. Meantime,
plants eavesdrop on insects,
feel the sound of water,
talk to one another.
             We humans never listen,
choose the knife, the arrow, sword or gun
and scare the blue tit balanced on the fuchsia bush.

Monument

"Words! Pens are too light.
Take a chisel to write" (BASIL BUNTING)

This northerner, who chiseled *Briggflatts*
from the Yorkshire dales, the Cumbrian fells,
inserted tender memory into hard experience,
this war-blown genius has planted all his passion
deep in Durham's Botanic Garden, carved on stone.

I want words chiseled in the throat of every leader,
peace letter bombs to calm the oceans of mistrust,
hope firecrackers to attack the dead wood stacked
by green and godly setting fuses hungry for a flame
to set Magnificat alight, blunt sentences that span
the space between the busy brain and weary heart.

Words! Hammer verbs that bump and bruise, thump
from a God who said "I make", and worlds became;
speaks "I am"—and words form what they mean;
who'll say "I do", to marry words to worlds and
chisel love from mouths now carved in stone.

Scotland

Miracles

"Tout commence en mystique, et tout finit en politique"　(Charles Péguy)

That secret sense
behind the skin,
the soul's adrenalin:
some say it kicks in rough,
full trot to canter; horse
or camel crunching gears.
I say it slips in silky,
as the pounding foot
feels for the grassy fell,
lungs full, windblown apprentice
wondering at his craft:
a miracle afoot.

A Dundee festival,
a diamond mirrorball,
it hung our hopes in space
thick as the darkness
in the ancient church.
Below, on stage
the music built a generation,
loath to lead, but rising
to creation out of nothing,
sweated hologram
touching street level:
a miracle down there.

Conversations
on the future
shape of Scotland:
key notes struck,
tuned to the times.
And then the Parliament
—what a start to pick apart
a scandal loss of sovereignty.
So as *our three tongued nation*
learned to sing again,
we lifted blinking eyes
and smiled at miracles.

St Mary's Haddington at Night

We listen silent, scattered round the church.
Candles flicker, high lights pick out arch and pillar.
Music jostles major, minor keys, just like
the story of this place, Burnt Candlemas,
Rough Wooing by King Henry Eighth,
that rest half ruined till the great rebuilding.

The bells are quiet at this hour of night:
they hang like metal sloths, asleep.
This is a special period, a holy space
to let the stones embrace our prayers,
fold them with care, lift them up to God
and hold them for a coming age.

To be "the solace of a whole community",
this Lamp of Lothian; squat temple
for the town, a house of grace
for wounded souls and worried hearts,
with sacrament, rejoicing and remembrance
at our life transitions, birth and death.

We listen silent, scattered round the church,
more ready now to face the music of our age,
its sharps and flats which sound our days.
We will get up, go home, calmer than before,
thankful for this unforced rhythm keeping
us in time and touch with greater things.

Saltire

Two planes crossed, and left a saltire in the sky.
Below, twelve centuries have flown by
since Angus King of Picts first saw it, and St Andrew
dropped into our history.

Elshinford now guards the flag;
the saltire names a literary award;
the banner links patriot and nationalist,
both proud of all our history.

A flag, a vision. War and peace, and ever since
the local squabbles about governance—
lily white or spectrum, royal blue or different hue:
they complicate our history.

John MacCormick raised his *Flag in the Wind* in print;
now it's gone all digital—but where
are folk like David Lyndsay, John McGrath
to set alight our history?

Two planes crossed, and left a saltire in the sky.
Below, the century is crawling by,
uncertain of its symbols. Who will write another
satire on our history?

This poem celebrates The Saltire Centre in Athelstaneford. See also Notes at the back.

Luik til the Burds o the Lift

"Good morning, theologians"—quo Martin Luther tae the burds
MATTHEW 6 V.26

Wechty thochts, primpit in gled rags, waffed
it waggies wha kin beck an jouk frae stane tae stane
an aiblins see a glisk o sun licht up oor mirkie minds.
Thir burd-harns hap frae Wittenburg tae Glesca,
or whaurever lugs ur preened, lik Luther,
teen on sae muckle bi a reidbreist ur a wrannie.

Heize yer bunnet til the lift thit's fu wi burds,
tweet the lair frae howe o hairt, aye, ding it oot,
than wap yer doots roon spirl an shoots
sae speugs kin big thir nests wi leal howp
an seal im sauf wi kinch o luve: aye,
thase wha yap kin larn tae flee yince mair.

Wha lilts his laud inti the keek o ilka day,
wha thraws his poesie abune the aigle's weeng,
whill thochty fowk will dab it wurds an waff
thur buiks fur tent? Jist lat the duikins paidle
tae collogue, rype thur nebs intil the reeve,
lift an lay the grace, queeple Amen.

lift: air, sky; *aiblins*: perhaps; *harns*: brains; *heize*: lift
kinch: knot; *laud*: praise; *duikin*: duckling; *tent*: attention
collogue: discussion; *reeve*: chatter; *queeple*: quack

How Things Are

"If you want messages, go to Safeway"   (Norman MacCaig)

No messages, said Norman, flyting with MacDiarmid
was it—more likely ministers, or maybe with himself,
he was so good at praising what things are
and leaving what they might be to philosophers,
without a strident "should be this" or "must be that".

I hear ice crack, and oceans short of breath, hard
data queueing up as methane bubbles out, and
metaphors ride bottles on our beaches, packed
with pleas from stranded birds and bleaching coral:
kill the plastic, ban the loggers, leave the coal aground.

The 'is' of science and 'maybe' of art link arms
to fill the human 'ought' with teeth so sharp
that modern messaging might prick the skin
of politicians, kick the shins of every one
to whack the pain of earth into our bones.

Flyting: a contest in mutual abuse between poets who respect each other

Tones of Destiny

I want to listen to our storied language,
wake, remember who I am;
I want to know our stacked up history
I want a hope for the unborn.

I want St Andrew's simple bread and fish
to feed a million Scottish throats;
I want Queen Margaret's skill at politics
I want old John the Common Weal.

I want to read and write without a censor,
access poetry and art,
I want the axe which split de Bohun's skull,
I want the light Columba found.

I want the magic of an island ceilidh
celebrating toil and play;
I want a life that someone notices,
I want to take *some* public step.

I want the craft of Bellany and Burns,
the nous of Hume, the sense of Reid;
I want the music Robert Carver spun,
I want horizons to be bright.

I want the faithfulness Jane Haining showed
to those who faced the Auschwitz smoke;
I want a God who is not deaf or dumb,
I want to voice my own requests.

I want the mind that James Clerk Maxwell had
to integrate his faith and thought;
I want the punch of Spark and Connolly,
I want the subtle Rankin twist.

I want to honour men like yon Keir Hardie,
stand with women seeking space;
I want to offer Mary Slessor praise,
I want some footsteps I can fill.

I want to race with Liddell, Hoy; dream on
with George MacDonald, Murray Grieve;
I want enough to give to other folk,
I want to lose and find myself.

I want a Government which knows the time
for referenda and for prayer;
I want to see the coming light of dawn,
I want a modest nation, wise and free.

Inchcolm

Join the cacophony of gulls, teenagers,
plumage whitening round the neck,
dressing for the dance their elders
choreograph a thousand times
until they drop and join the litter
which infests this trampled island.

Ride the humming wave of tourists
breaking in multi-coloured foam
with a flotilla of footwear, light
for such a weight of curiosity;
dark and light-skinned, with a titter
of tongues to probe this listening island.

See through the raggle of styles,
roofs rough-stoned and stepped;
a peppering of plaques among the ruins,
iron ship with sail set for the wind
above the chapter house; a glitter
of sun to fleck this sombre island.

And then:
a genesis of quiet,
an exodus of tourists,
this testament of earth and angels,
everywhere a memory of holiness.

In Response to Bible Texts

Incarnation

"For though the Lord is high, he regards the lowly"   Psalm 138 v.6

Soaring space
vanishes into metaphor;
high and low span
this divine care plan,
texted in psalm,
shaped in Mary's womb:
pride unhorsed,
humility endorsed,
all open before
the lightning flash of God
who earths his hero
at ground zero.

Beating on the Door

"How long, O Lord? Will you forget me forever?" Psalm 13 v.1

I'm beating, God, upon your door.
I screw my eyes to read your lips
but I am shaken to the core

by conflict, climate, and what's more
you've morphed into a God who sleeps
when I would worship and adore.

On glib response I set no store
nor on those charismatic cantrips
which have left me raw and sore.

How long before I rant and roar,
or worse, when my whole being slips
to shadow life upon the floor

I will ooze death through every pore
while casually the Devil rips
my fading faith to shreds. Therefore

I'm beating, God, upon your door;
with these mantraps I'll get to grips;
I'm pounding, Lord, upon your door
and I *will* worship and adore.

Cantrip: spell or trick

Shepherd Sonnet PSALM 23

Contradictions, with a sudden mirk
to overtake our brash faith, our rosy
hopes. The unexpected snakes devour
the flimsy ladders that we think so firm
for easy climbs to happiness. Who knows,
we might today be falling, calling out
for God to hear us—hold us, help us, fold us
God into those arms that felt the blows
that hammered nails through flesh. Your love can meet
the cost of shepherding the likes of us,
and give us courage in the cold of night,
the daytime heat, the struggles of the street.

You fill my empty cup with hope again:
the yes and no of life become 'Amen'.

Enemies

"Fight against those who fight against me!"   Psalm 35 v.1

When it is too easy to say
'Love your enemies'
When it is repugnant to say
'Love your enemies'
When it is impossible to say
'Love your enemies'

I shall seize this great aggressive psalm
I shall load it with these righteous bullets
I shall smile and slip the safety catch
     and—oh God—
You stepped into the line of fire
nodding your head at my complaint
opening your heart to all my anger
holding your hands up in surrender

The Cosmic Synagogue

"They think a deadly thing has fastened on me . . . even my bosom friend, in whom I trusted, has lifted the heel against me."   Psalm 41 vv.8–9

You would expect to hear the word amen
within the mosque or church or synagogue;
the cosmic record shows, for rich and poor,
throughout our history the road is hard,
the way is narrow, dogged by human snakes
who trip and trap the worship of the blest.

While prayers and psalms preoccupy the blest
who long to see a cosmic great amen
transforming every sloth and slug and snake
into the dolphins of the synagogue,
the savvy sigh: they know how really hard
it is to change the asset-rich, time-poor.

Cosmic is as cosmic does; the poor
survive on scattered crumbs among the blest
and wish for more than words; it's hard
for broken refugees to say "Amen"
and "Praise the Lord" when synagogues
of every faith play racist cards with snakes.

With just a touch of irony, the snake's
acknowledged as a sign of healing, poor
joke for the sick within the synagogue
who think that healing's in the deal, a blest
bonanza for our rapturous amen:
a package with no comfort—just too hard.

To hold together different worlds is hard,
to keep believing humming birds and snakes
both share a cosmic plan, to say amen
to theft of time and assets, seems a poor
and dour response, when dozens of the ablest
minds have banned snakes from the synagogue.

So who is welcome in the synagogue
to sing these psalms? Should I include those hard
unholy enemies of mine, say "Blest
are you" regardless if you're saint or snake,
a sloth or slug, labelled rich or poor?
And while I pray, I hear them hiss, "Amen".

This cosmic synagogue has snakes
who make it hard for all, even the poor,
to say "Blest be the Lord: Amen, Amen!"

Longing   Psalm 84

Every leaf lassoes the life of heaven,
tells its story, death and resurrection
whirling through the galaxies, from worm
to star, each whispering a silent tune
that found a voice in Jesus, Mary's son,
who made his earthly pilgrimage a psalm,
a praise and prayer oblation in the temple
that we rightly call our universe.

We pass our days through better and through worse,
while sparrows nest and swallows raise their young;
we find hope springing in our desert days,
and hold the doors for God in storm and calm.

How long before he comes, and all things move
towards their place? How strong the call above!

Fair and Square   Psalm 119

No tapestry complete without a square
jaw somewhere, to remind tame images
that words do more than chatter,
show how *torah* draws a frame for life
to challenge slipshod needlework,
set out certain things that matter.

No book complete without some ordering
of chapters, sequences of numbers, letters
sailing A to Z, the blacks, the whites,
all shades of tighter *petit point* let loose
upon a canvas sea, like decorated buoys
which mark each passage with eight riding lights.

No symphony complete without a switch
from law to liberty, a swatch of tones,
an itch unwrapped so strings rehearse
its secret. Bless you, ancient makar, shrewd
composer, artist, stitcher: you have left
your needle prints so clear in every verse.

No life complete without God's art and music
hidden in our sober prose, artless, silent,
waiting for the word to waken, say hello,
and introduce a new dimension, dancing
intimacy to the edge of long horizons,
splashing colour on a great allegro.

A Proverb Reconsidered Proverbs 6 v.6

Tracking wild across the Sierra Nevada,
the ants are in God's eye, a little armada
of twitching purpose, joyfully numbered,
since one ant is worth a thousand elephants
in heaven's economy. Even one dumb bird
is not an oxymoron, and God (for instance)
puts a single anthill on the same sure
footing as a skyscraper, because they share
the solid earth and need the same pure
air. With God one single petal is as fair
as any grand bouquet, two nanometres
rank beside two thousand metres.

How to recalibrate our thought
is something urgent that we ought
to do. For if an insignificant ant
can ferry something twenty times its size
with giant energy, keep constant
witness to God's algebra, surprise
us all with tricks of geo-engineering,
then we need to get down on our knees
and see through God's own lens, peering
at these little creatures and their cities,
nests of enterprise; for God is adamant,
and tells us slugs, "Observe the ant!"

The Golden Rule

"In everything do to others as you would have them do to you"
MATTHEW 7 V.12

I am tired of those who polish up the golden rule
until they see their own reflection smiling at them.
Bored by their books, their habits unhelpful,
peeved at their practice, astounded by assumptions,
    I would like:
a love that looks with favour on enquiry,
a love that lends a hankie to my tears,
a love that launches boats, not liners,
a love that listens to my hopes and fears.

If I were them, I'd love to read this poem,
change my thinking, beat my breast a bit,
read different books, adopt better habits,
modify my practices, draw new conclusions.
    But I need:
a love that makes more radical enquiry
a love that manages to feel their pain,
a love that lets them choose the ground,
a love that loves, and loves again.

The Father's Hands Luke 15 vv.11–32

From Rembrandt's painting, 'The Return of the Prodigal'

Each hand thumbed, four-fingered
yet—strangely separate;
two angled tracks for love
to rest on penitent shoulders.
Father and mother love, combined
in one whose welcome tells us
all we need to know of God.

His brother's hands stay folded
firm inside his cloak of piety—
but those are not the hands of God
who finds new ways to reach
the heart of everyone who kneels.

The Lord's Breakfast   John 21 vv.1–13

She builds a fire with beach sticks,
sets it alight on the lounge carpet
with a bright red cloth, beyond
the pebbled scattering of sand,
the waving blue gossamer sea
jumping with tiny glass fish.

She tells a tale of seven men,
lost at losing their best friend.
Their empty night at sea, fishing
memories, catching questions
Sunrise, and a voice inviting them
to make their failure public news.

She brings to life the eighth man,
who knows the sea and those who fish;
she calls them to his breakfast,
sings a grace and breaks a loaf,
shares a meal that lets the fish man
weave the carpet of our lives.

Swimming Lessons from Gaza

"He plunged into the promise"   ROMANS 4 V.20 IN *THE MESSAGE*

No wild swimming in the desert, Abraham,
but I guess the metaphor could borrow
from your childhood dips in the Euphrates.

Blessing—like a well beneath the sand,
a spring sea-salted with the faithfulness of God
to nurse a child, to birth a land and people.

Promise—recognized by Bible and Qu'ran—
which makes this land 'prepared' for Abraham's people,
but who today deserves this holy pledge?

We gaze aghast at Abraham's warring children
claiming that the pool they fill with blood
is theirs alone, when once a prophet said

God could make Abraham's heirs rise up from stones:
much more from flesh and blood—could Muslims, Jews
and Christians share the land, plunge into promise?

The Hourglass   1 Corinthians 10 v.4

We hardly notice how the sand grains pass
our lives, our loves so quickly through the glass;
until that tipping point, we stay cocooned
within a nest of circumstance, attuned
to family noise, the grunts and little farts
that make dull symphony, their counterparts
within the crowd just sounding much the same;
no obvious fuss, no rush to praise or blame
until the shuffle shifts its paradigm.
Suddenly we all run out of time,
and fall apart. It's then God flips the scene
to let us see what all the pieces mean,
and how each tiny grain's a universe
to be explored, for better—not for worse—
and how in every running grain of sand
God travels with us to the promised land.

Change   REVELATION 21

When night is day, and day is night
when earth is heaven, heaven earth,
when all the wrong is put to right
then time and space will have new birth.

When earth is heaven, heaven earth,
and honey bees buzz city streets,
then time and space will have new birth
and truth defeat all counterfeits.

While honey bees buzz city streets
rough sleepers walk the countryside,
then truth defeats all counterfeits,
old maids are young as any bride.

Rough sleepers walk the countryside
with Adam, Eve themselves again,
old maids are young as any bride
and cry with joy instead of pain.

With Adam, Eve themselves again,
the poor as rich, the rich as poor,
they'll cry with joy instead of pain,
their life secure, their future sure.

With poor as rich, and rich as poor,
and cities architects' delight—
their life secure, their future sure
and God's intention full in sight.

With cities architects' delight
then night is day, and day is night;
when God's intention's full in sight
then all the wrong is put to right.

Scent from Patmos REVELATION 1 VV.9–20

Patmos: island cabin of my present past,
full of windows opening memories,
the life of Christ pure incense, embracing
praying friends who know my fate

and keep me minded; gentle warriors
who blow back the smoke of Caesar
smothering me with lies, to kill my senses
and my prophecy. Scent of sea, my prison,

every tide a jailer teasing me upon the ebb
with false release, and telling me again
upon the flow that Caesar rules. I see
the shore, I smell the wind that moves
across that sea, but here I stay and swing
a censer with my prayers: so dream I will.

I write my vision, shape my smell, unfold
my ears on purpose for this message to the seven:
Letters crafted from the furnishings of heaven—
stars, and sword, and waterfalls—pictures
ploughed into the soil of pagan cities,
to bear harvest in my time, and times to come.

Seven lampstands and their oil lit up for God.
What smoke? The pure, sweet incense of a faithful
company? The acrid stench of compromise?
The half-rich, tired scent of love gone cool?

My nose, my ear, my eye lie dead before you.
Lift me, give me life in every sense
that I may breathe and smell the air of heaven,
cross the sea that pounds me into exile,
taste the word that reconnects me to
my future; post these letters to your people.

Questions

Consequences

Sometimes you see a flush of leaves,
but even Eden did not plant itself.
I imagine God in shirt sleeves,
pondering a fresh dug patch, a shelf
of seedling fruit trees at the ready.

Adam's largely ignorant of himself,
Eve still tries to catch God's eye,
in blissful ignorance of what a skelf
from one wide branching moral tree
would pierce her skin, and prick myself.

Bible Shopping

Folk who want a simple God of love,
nice-tasting food, not dumps of sin,
have fled from Bible, Sundays, clergy, churches.

Why read such awful books as Exodus,
Egyptian babies, Pharaoh's troops all dead,
with God presented executioner?

Why suffer ancient battles, law codes, gore
and vengeance, when a quick flip through to Jesus
puts an easy, smiling face on God?

Why not chop, redact the nasty bits,
cut out the cruel cross, or keep it just
a sign of love somewhere in spite of all?

Why not? Life is not a dish of roses,
violence not beyond the reach of God,
nor death the end of every human dream.

Why not? New is just as tough as Old,
its sense a package with a thread unbroken
by our shopping, chopping, knocking habits.

Why not? Jesus kept Passover meal,
and wore our human worst upon his skin
—yes, Jesus ploughed up hell for all of us.

Celebrating Life

"*L'Hayyim*" you call, and raise life's cloudy glass
to toast the God who likes to shift his shape
but leave a finger print, perhaps a glint
of something extra. "Read my lips," God says,
and disappears behind a joke, a cry, a puff of smoke
that drifts across our week and leaves a hint
of heaven, wrapped in all this business filling
hearts and daily meetings, mouths and ordinary time.

Four good white teeth, where Sacks' profile laughs
at letters gilding that last paperback;
teeth and tongue that caught a grace on the wind
of God, that chewed a grape draped casually
upon an ornament, placed to rescue protocol
and show God mischievously there, unfazed
by all these lunching Presidents and Premiers,
just happy to relax within a bunch of grapes.

"God lives where we allow him in," said Rabbi Mendel.
Hard to get a handle on this temple-trotting God,
who sits at table in the human house of prayer
we call ourselves, and breathes a whisper
or a quiet whistle somewhere unexpected.
There is an art of happiness, a silent voice
that smiles around the edges of the canvas
littered with the bundled progress of each day.

L'Hayyim (or *L'Chaim*) is the traditional Jewish toast "to Life!"

Discovery

Imagine finding God after all those years,
lodged like *Endurance*, waiting against the odds
below the ice of unbelief. No touching, but
at least we know there are no bodies in the tomb.
Like Shackleton, God must have abandoned ship,
surrendered reputation and the relics of his glories,
taken his disciples on that dreadful journey
all across Antarctica to reach Ukraine, and all
those places where the risky story of creation
plays uncensored on the wide screens of the world.

Chance and calculation are adrift upon the ice
that bears the weight of love, and sacrifice.

Do not Put 'Gentle' onto God

after Dylan Thomas

Do not put 'gentle' onto God
in such a violent universe
unless you have a lightning rod.

Call God cruel, sadist, sod,
or some expletive even worse:
do not put 'gentle' onto God

or 'meek and mild', or 'friendly bod',
and OMG is just perverse
unless you have a lightning rod.

Search for a gentle man who had
the heart and guts to bear the curse.
Do not put 'gentle' onto God

if you're avoiding all things bad,
or try to write this kind of verse
unless you have a lightning rod.

Just find a chosen human, glad
to put the gear into reverse.
Do not put 'gentle' onto God
unless you have a lightning rod.

Reaching for It

"Show us again some end to shape our storyline"
(Micheal O'Siadhail, 'Stretching')

Brave poet, fed up with the gush
and clever claptrap of our day
which sits and preens on social media
till the next small clutch of items
rushes in to snap up standing.

Brave wayfarer, keen to skylark
listening to his own heart beat
a pulse, spark fire within the skin
of stories left upon a shelf
and marked "religion—do not touch".

Brave God, who gives the shelf a shape
and waits to see who leaves the crowd
with curious fingers, pulls herself
up to the rim of what we know
and edges eyes and ears wide open.

Brave everyone, when lifetime habits
clatter to the floor, to shift
the paradigm, to show our age
is coming to its end, not mere
extinction, but respect for God

which grounds our wisdom, keeps our minds
from shelving purpose. Love is there
all unexpected, pouring heaven
to earth, whenever jars of pride
are broken, long lost stories spoken.

God Chatter

*"We jump from picture to picture, and cannot follow
the living curve that is breathlessly the same"*   (Louis MacNiece)

Breathlessly the same. No serpent's fire,
no wolfish pant or howl, no lion's breath
to give a whiff of danger, scratch of ire;

but breathless is no euphemistic death,
no loss of grip, no lack of spark or wit,
no test of loyalty, no shibboleth;

instead it gives us God's identikit
as waiter, watcher, blowing in the air
a cloud of bubbles, what will come of it

God wonders, leaving humans with a flair
for prophecy to plunder graphic files,
or excavate another subtle layer

of Bible soil to fix in frozen piles.
Stay breathless with a God who could complete
the Ironman, then add a thousand miles,

but says, "Been there, long before you;" so delete
that option, click on "Do you want to see
a wave with Plato surfing on his feet

with Paul Celan?" or "Would you rather be
an eagle with a taste for chocolate,
Benedetti in the groove, or me?"

God chattering is more than just a bit
of poetry, but taken to the wire
our world is breathless, ripe for some of it.

.

Mind Maps

"You reside in my memory" (AUGUSTINE, *CONFESSIONS*, 10.24.35)

Eerie quote, that, out of context:
tweak the temporal lobe and out God goes,
no need to wait on time's dementing.

I want to pull Augustine from his study chair,
pick up the saintly man, turn him upside down,
shake his pockets till his memories tumble
into the holy hags of heaven, lodged in a Mind
that logs each whisper, knows each whimper,
all our brilliance and our break ups bagged.

Or should we seek nirvana, God's divine dementia,
space-time emptied of each earthly niggle, memory
a stream run dry, a slate wiped clean, a frozen screen?
Who wants to keep the jagged scores of Partick Thistle
or the passing rant and roar of propaganda? Why not
give earth's commonplace a shuffle into nothingness?

Bring back the books that open on the day of judgment,
catch the butterfly that flicks its blue into my face,
file photos of the kingfisher, the kudu and the cobra.
I want to know that every tick is counted somewhere,
every crumb is eaten by a hungry dog, each glance
is caught, remembered, tracked and traced to source.

Deep questions, these, in any context:
probe too seriously, and in God comes,
our wise or wild mind maps frequenting.

Poems of Time and Season

Nothing Much

Nothing is impossible—already,
double-dealing in a phrase—
whatever nothing is.
But take that word play
back to base, *creatio ex nihilo*:
what wonderful confusion,
wormy holes of meaning
may bed science and theology,
for ever yoked as yang and yin.

Coincidence

"When I pray, coincidences happen"   (Archbishop William Temple)

The lorry coincided with our space:
break time, and rhyming with 'collided'.

Later, we debate if it's coincidence
when a friend came, ended up beside us

right on cue. She was two cars in front—
praying? Or just swearing at the queue,

stationary, till that squeal of brakes:
sharp shunt, a noisy dunt to any meditation

on collision, accidents of heaven and earth
perhaps; but maybe gaps appear in our precision,

lost light energies we never thought
were there, until a prayer brought faith to sight.

Was it happenstance that she was close
and looked back, took us home: just chance?

Advent

Year-end anchor, liturgical rope
which ties one year to the next:
strange month, haunted by hope,

loud with chime and carol, subtext
scolding us to heed that air-brushed
angst of expectation, which bisects

our scrambled list of tasks, crushed
into December's crucible. Take
instead each day-gift, now unrushed

by shopping, phone or Christmas cake,
and listen while those hidden sounds
vibrate your heart-strings. Make

a pilgrimage of Advent, do the rounds
of charity in unexpected places;
flex your muscles, break the bounds

of all those stereo-typefaces
that obscure true Advent graces.

Advent Thoughts

I thought to wait it out, this Advent,
let the busyness pass by, enjoy
the calm of age, an empty stage, content
to make the space my private toy.

But soon I knew I had to let it in,
do face to face instead of watching Zoom,
eye Jesus as my coming next of kin,
let others share my waiting room.

For time runs into everyone's affairs,
reset upon the road to Bethlehem,
when God prepared to take our human cares,
to wear our clothes, and model them.

Epiphany

Hold up the sky, work through the night
to bring to life an ancient theme:
the centuries will cradle light.

The stars may fall, climate backbite
and chew and spit us all downstream.
Hold up the sky, work through the night.

The challenges seem infinite,
but once a baby made it seem
the centuries can cradle light.

The rich delight in sitting tight,
but truth destroys such self-esteem.
Hold up the sky, work through the night.

We know too much, too late. Hindsight
betrays us, makes us want to scream
"The centuries must cradle light!"

The magi will come back to sight
and share their old, forgotten dream:
hold up the sky, work through the night,
the centuries will cradle light.

Holy Saturday

This is the day we dive, dodge the stone-edged pieties
on either side, the hard print of the holy. We go
for the dark matter dredging spiritualities
of East and West, the worm holes of revenge and war
which bore into Kyiv, eat out Jerusalem,
evading media and beasting sanity; they outlaw the least
hint of hope, certain they have stopped the calendar,
made this a day to twist, unpick all certainties,
spatter religion with the acid rain of what is really
going on . . . the day when faith is what it is,
the guarantee of things not seen, the gift
and pledge of one who braved the graveyard shift.

The End of It

Just so many days remain and, wishing exercise
with little pain, I'm on an old and easy path. My eyes
are focused on a creature carrying its carapace:
it's bent—or should I say stretched out—on challenging my space.
"Welcome, snail," I say, "you may postpone your fate
if my boot's careful, and my gaze is straight."

Just so many days remain and, mounting difficulties
fall like hail on every government. The forecast is
not good: "Events, dear boy," Macmillan said when I was young,
they smash the shell of competence we grow. When time has rung
the bell on those in power, who knows what kind of weather
will face man and mollusc, fur and feather?

Just so many days remain and, fronting all of us
a metaphor we recognize, that silent final bus
which every poet deals with differently, though none evade
the track's dead end, that gives glib preacher men their stock in trade.
Did I say, "Welcome, snail"? That's how we live and die,
our small attentions edging out the why.

Just so many days remain—and counting, so we say,
while hoping that the pun will keep significance in play.
The snail knows not the meaning of the foot that might avoid it,
the human knows a whole lot more, and often can't abide it.
So we choose: MacDiarmid's wheel, or Herbert's promise,
or the old age rage of Dylan Thomas.

Old

in memory of the Revd Jim Powrie

His lips are open,
moving, as they whisper
"You must stay for tea."
Hospitality a habit
of that holy lifetime,
now a quiet question
on his warm wax face,
hollowed out by age
and supplication.

Fresh

Fresh, each letter dancing slow strathspeys
on ageing skin, unused to such attention,
wondering what the future holds.

Fresh, a sibilant for every person
spelling something yet unread, a promise
waiting to be understood.

Fresh, heuristic sound to offer dreams
for everyone who walks and combs our beaches,
climbs our hills, lives in our cities.

Fresh, a hope-word smiling from a grave
which once gave hospitality to Jesus,
opened to his claim on life.

Fresh, an art which papers walls in heaven
with life-forming fragrance, scent to fill
the hearts of all who long for more.

Heaven to Go

"Heaven in ordinarie . . . something understood" (George Herbert)

"What's the go of it?" (James Clerk Maxwell)

So how does heaven work, beyond the harps,
the golden streets, the clouds, beyond
St Peter at the gate, the flats, the sharps?

I recall the Emigrant who said,
"I'll show you heaven: don't look up,
look round about you, like a child, instead."

Curious, I put it to the test;
I sent my senses scribbling, free
of prejudice; sat back with interest;

noticed, in the corner of this room,
the cupboard where the memories
put those we cherish back into the womb

to be reborn when time is riddled, good
is salvaged, and the honesty
stuck in that vase is round the neighbourhood.

Or contemplate that picture on the wall,
a woman watching, hands in prayer,
a kettle on the fire, and most of all

she wonders how to offer her poor life
and circumstance to God, who might
transform the world as well as that goodwife.

My feet are on that modest carpet, blown
by several thousand steps and scrapes,
ready for its colours to be shown.

Heaven's in that pile of clothes, whose hope
is something more than landfill, longing
to be fit to wrap up prince and pope.

Beside them is that pelargonium,
wondering what unknown scents
would fill and fire a future cranium.

I can imagine phones which know the place
of fellowship and silence, a line
hot-charged with wonder, getting through: that's grace.

Above me is a plain brass ring of five
lamps, not of six or four, because
all art needs something different to thrive

and like that woman here beside me
makes it new each day, so that
I know how heaven's quite extraordinary.

Sky Talk

    This evening
it began with sky:
grey rags flying
across the blue,
under crumpled
cirrus clouds,
furtive flag
of what's to come,
an opening gambit
in a wordless video.

    Tomorrow
it will end with sky,
the books of science
warn us, and the seers
nod. The files unseal,
and resurrection
clears the attic.
A taller story
raises rag and bone
to more than we can know.

Occupation

"God has exiled me from myself" (Sweeney Astray, by Seamus Heaney)
"God is closer than myself" (Augustine)

Space-shifting God,
you push the universe to wild frontiers,
you spin the plates of planets till they fall
and life appears, clinging to their rims.

Mind-shifting God,
you ride the pulsing world within
our fragile bodies, as our spirits fail
and shelf-life shortens, exile beckons.

Shape-shifting God,
you pick the moment, deck the process,
occupy our scattered bits of self
and pin up signs of more to come.

Notes

'Blue in Flodigarry'. Written beside my wife Margaret, who was painting the view over to the mainland from the home of the Gaelic poet Maoilios Caimbeul.

'Cosmic Marriage'. Basil Bunting was an English poet who published his long poem 'Briggflatts' in 1966.

'Miracles'. The epigraph from Charles Péguy comes from his book *Notre Jeunesse* published in 1910. It was cited by George MacLeod (in English) in his book *One Way Left*, published in 1956. British Sign Language is now a fourth official language in Scotland alongside English, Gaelic and Scots.

'St Mary's Haddington at Night'. The church suffered at the hands of Edward III in 1355 ('The Burnt Candlemas'), and later during Henry VIII's 'rough wooing'—the 16th century Anglo-Scottish wars.

'Saltire'. Elshinford is the local pronunciation of the name of the village of Athelstaneford. *Ane Satyre of the Thrie Estaitis* was written by Sir David Lyndsay, more recently *The Cheviot, the Stag and the Black, Black Oil* by John McGrath.

'The Father's Hands'. Rembrandt's painting is in a gallery in St Petersburg, and is the subject of Henri Nouwen's book *The Return of the Prodigal*.

'Celebrating Life'. The eponymous book by Jonathan Sacks was published by Harper Collins in 2000; Sacks was Chief Rabbi of the United Hebrew Congregations of the British Commonwealth from 1991 to 2013. Rabbi Menachem Mendel was also known as the Kotzker Rebbe.

'Mind Maps'. Partick Thistle are a Scottish football team known as 'The Jags'.

'The End of It'. MacDiarmid's wheel refers to his long poem 'A Drunk Man Looks at the Thistle'. George Herbert seldom if ever uses the actual word 'promise' but so many of his poems (like 'The Invitation' or 'The Glance') are full of it.

'Do Not Put "Gentle" onto God'. The Dylan Thomas reference is to his villanelle 'Do not go Gentle into that Good Night'.

'Coincidence'. Margaret and I remain grateful to Carol Marples who very kindly took us home after our road accident just north of Berwick.

'Old'. The Revd Jim Powrie was minister of Chalmers Ardler Church in Dundee when we lived there, and at the time of writing was resident in Haddington.

'Heaven to Go'. The Herbert epigraph is from the first of his poems on 'Prayer' in *The Complete Works*; the Clerk Maxwell one refers to what the famous Scottish scientist used to ask when he was a boy (see Bruce Ritchie's book, *James Clerk Maxwell: Faith, Church and Physics*, published by Handsel Press in 2024).

Acknowledgments

A number of these poems have appeared in booklets, in my 2022 book, *Temple and Tartan: Psalms, Poetry and Scotland*, or been published by *Acumen*, the *Free Church Record*, *London Grip*, *Participatio*, *Poetry Scotland*, and *Scintilla*. 'Tones of Destiny' won a ScottishPEN prize for writing to celebrate the 700th anniversary of the Treaty of Arbroath. 'Fair and Square' is included in the 2024 anthology, *Scottish Religious Poetry*.

I'm grateful to Jim Tedrick and Matt Wimer of Wipf and Stock for their advice and courtesy, and for their willingness to accept a book of poetry with UK spelling.

I would like to thank Harry Smart very warmly for his advice in the selection and editing of these poems, and for his generous Introduction. A few were written during a recent Glasgow University PhD in the field of 'theology and creative practice', and I thank Doug Gay and Alan Riach for their mentoring, and further back the poet Roger Garfitt. Before that I'm also grateful to Brenda Lealman and the Creative Arts Retreat Movement who accidentally got me writing poetry when as their treasurer I felt duty bound to go to a retreat and chose 'poetry' somewhat at random. All part of God's gracious providence.

Jock Stein, June 2025

www.ingramcontent.com/pod-product-compliance
Lightning Source LLC
Chambersburg PA
CBHW060420050426
42449CB00009B/2053